Can't Sell, Won't Sell

Find out why you're not selling, how
to do it, what works and what
doesn't and how to have fun with it

Stuart Pearce

Finally, a book that doesn't try to reinvent the sales wheel.

Instead, it delivers refreshing ideas and concepts on how to maximise and implement your own sales potential!

Ben Caton, MD at SWSE & Wellmi

Chapter One

Understanding why and the ground rules.

Chapter Two

More of the basics and how to use them.

Chapter Three

Closing.

Chapter Four

Going Old School, First Impressions & Professor Albert.

Chapter Five

Using your Voice and some Tips and Tricks.

Chapter Six

Using the right Words, Influencing and Questioning.

Chapter Seven

Scripts, Preparation, Behaviour and your Aim.

Chapter Eight

Commit to it, Learn Your Craft, have a Plan.

Introduction

The things I'm going to tell you about in this book will work whether you're selling face to face or over the telephone.

There will be some obvious differences and I'll do my best to highlight them as we go through it.

Let's understand one thing straight off the bat. In today's sales environment, there are far more channels that you can use to get the elusive sale than there ever were 20 years ago, even 10 years ago.

We also need to understand that the end customer is different now, they generally don't want to waste time and they're more often than not, much more aware of the sales process than ever before.

On saying that and despite all the other channels and so on, people still like to talk to another person when spending their money – admittedly not every time, but still enough that having the skill to hold a conversation still matters.

Just to make everyone feel better, I am regularly told off for my reliance on Amazon for birthday presents etc but I blame the fact that I'm busy and it's convenient.

Chapter One

"Nothing happens until someone sells something"
Henry Ford

Why can't I sell?

I have been asked this question or variations of it many times over the years and there is no one answer, purely and simply because everyone is different, their approach is different and their level of ability is different (as is there resistance to sales)

People who start their own business generally do so because they are great at what they do and have a desire to do it for themselves rather than for someone else's benefit and of course to get the freedom that working for yourself can (apparently) give you – although those of us that made that leap know only too well that the freedom part comes much later!

Ponder on this for a moment, if I asked you to talk to someone and explain to them what it is that you do, you could undoubtedly keep that going for a while and not be overly concerned.

Now try it this way, talk to someone and explain to them what you do and then ask them to pay you to do it for them.

1

At this point most people go into panic, the butterflies in your stomach are doing somersaults and you start wondering how the heck you're going to manage it.

NO! I CAN'T BE BOTHERED TO SEE ANY PESKY SALESMAN....I'VE GOT A BATTLE TO FIGHT!

And therein lies the problem, what most people do is separate the two parts from each other. I have been on coaching calls and heard the person I'm coaching physically take a deep breath before they start their pitch.

What you need to do is make it one complete conversation. People worry so much about the sales part that they work themselves up into such a panic that the sales part falls to pieces and then they lose the sale – serving only to confirm that sales is horrible and they shouldn't do it anymore because it's horrible and sales people are the devil and people know what I do so they'll buy from me and anyway sales is horrible and...well you see where I'm going with this

We have something in our house that my Son finds

hilarious, which in its basic form is if we play a game and I can't do it, then it's a silly game – but then I am a salesman at heart and I like to win.

The reason I tell you this (aside from highlighting my own infallibility) is because when people who aren't trained in it fail at sales then they want someone or something to blame and sales is after all horrible – but it's always worth a quick look at yourself first.

I have many a conversation such as 'he's a born salesman' or 'it's because she's so confident' and so on. The fact remains that we're all born salespeople and have unlimited confidence, we just lose it as we get older by letting things get in the way or allowing people to persuade us otherwise.

Let me expand a smidgen,

Picture this, you're 5 years old and on holiday with your family, you want an ice cream so you put on your best cute face and ask your Mum. She's not particularly helpful and says no, so you resort to plan B and ask your Dad. He is after all usually a push over on such topics.

Unfortunately, he heard your Mum's response and promptly agrees with her (I know, the cheek of it, is he a man or a mouse?) do you give up there? Do you heck as like, plan C is drop to the floor delivering your finest 'I want an ice cream' tantrum until, shamed with embarrassment, they give in and buy you the aforementioned ice cream and thus all is well with the world once more.

That, folks, is sales in its purest form. You had a goal in mind, and you tried all the angles until you got the result you needed. You also fulfilled a need, the need your parents had for you to stop screaming so they could return to the relative quiet that comes with having a five-year-old.

Now let's be sensible here, if your prospective customer doesn't immediately agree to buy from you, I wouldn't suggest throwing yourself to the floor and throwing a tantrum until they say yes (funny, but not very helpful). The point I'm making here is that sales is about finding the customers need and (ideally) filling it with something you have.

The problem lies, as I mentioned, in that we lose this ability over the years.

So, no, there are not any born salespeople but there are people who are what we call a 'people person'. Someone with the ability to talk to others and make them feel at ease etc

Or are they just really well trained salespeople...

As you'd imagine, I do quite a lot of sales coaching and much of this is done with small business owners and people whose first choice of things to do is not sales.

When I do this type of coaching, the first thing I want to

do is get people used to the idea of sales and that's it's not a dirty word and actually quite easy to do if you know how.

What I've taken to doing lately is asking them to think about these three questions.

1. Are you good at what you do?

2. Do people benefit from what you sell them?

3. Can you sell it to your Best Friend and still be their Best Friend?

If you can answer Yes, Yes, Yes to these then you've got half the job done, the rest is just know how and believe me when I tell, by the time we've finished this book, you'll have that knowhow and you'll wonder what all the fuss is about. Let's take a moment to delve a little deeper into each of those questions.

1. Are you good at what you do?

Being good at what you do not only benefits you, but it also obviously benefits your clients. It also means that if you believe that you're good at what you do then you will have far more confidence in yourself when talking to prospective clients, which in turn means that you will sound so much better when talking to them.

2. Do people benefit from what you sell them?

This one may sound a little bit obvious but whoever you're selling to needs to have and see the benefits of what you've got, otherwise it's going to be a fairly pointless and short conversation. And again it's back to your belief in yourself and the product/service you have. Will it make things easier for them or more efficient or more cost effective and so on.

3. Can you sell it to your Best Friend etc?

I've talked about belief in the product/service and in yourself and if you don't have that, if and when you sell it to someone you will feel horrible. On the other hand, if you do have that belief then when you sell to somebody, you will know you've done the right thing, for them and for you.

So, to look at the questions again.

1. Are you good at what you do?

2. Do people benefit from what you sell them?

3. Can you sell it to your Best Friend and still be their friend?

It may not be the most profound set of questions, but it will still make you think enough about your approach and about what you're doing to give you a good place to start.

OK, let's get down to business. As with anything in life that you want to be successful at, you need to build a good foundation (I'm sure we all remember the 'built a house on the sand' story from school) so with that in mind, we're going to take a look at the basics.

Once you have a handle on the basics and you can do them without thinking, everything else will just fall into place. In fact, with sales, if you can master the basics, the rest is just having a conversation.

1. Preparation

Preparation is key, you can't just take a run at it and hope for the best. Well you can if you wish, but you're more likely to just fall on your face, have a bunch of people miffed at you and you'll have very little in the way of sales, if any.

Preparation in sales is about knowing what you want to get out of the conversation you're going to have. Think about the end result you'd like to get.

Remind yourself of the three questions we talked about.

Once you've got that in your head, the preparation continues. Think about the person or persons you are going to speak to, what business they are involved in, what you can offer them.

Let's look at that last one for a minute.

What can you offer them?

The best way to approach this one is to think in terms of what pain points do they have and how can you fix them.

Pain points are things that cause you trouble. It doesn't matter what it is, is just something that causes you to work extra time or spend extra money etc that you'd rather not have to.

Your job as the 'salesperson' is to find out what their 'pain points' are and then offer them a solution – all while having what seems to them like a non-salesy conversation, remembering the basics and all the good stuff about your product/service – easy right.

One of the easiest ways to work out how to fix their pains points is by understanding your features and benefits, but don't panic, we'll get to those in a minute.

So to reiterate, preparation is key. Preparing properly will mean that you deliver a good solid presentation, you'll be able to answer any questions with confidence and your prospective customer will believe and trust you.

"Your prospective customer will believe and trust you"

Just let that sink in for a moment…

Something we need to appreciate and understand in sales is that it doesn't matter if your product/service is the best ever and that your pricing is fantastic. If the person doesn't believe what you're saying and/or doesn't trust you then it won't matter one bit.

In sales, trust is everything.

2. Features and Benefits

The idea behind features and benefits is a fairly easy one but it is so often used in the wrong way.

So, first things first, let's see if we can establish the difference between the two and clear up any confusion.

Features are the list of contents on the box, they're the things that your product does, the technical side if you like.

In simple terms, it's logic.

Benefits are what you gain from having that certain product or service. It's the 'what's in it for me'.

To balance it out, benefits is the emotion.

People do not buy on logic, they buy on emotion. So it carries that they don't buy the features, they buy the benefits.

The train of thought may start out with logic but I assure you, the final decision is always based on emotion.

For example, you're walking down the street and you have an urge for a bar of chocolate. So you pop into the closest shop and you're faced with rows of choices. The logical thing to do is to pick up the nearest bar and buy that one. Simple.

But that's not what you do is it. You look at the choices and you take out the ones you don't like or don't particularly fancy at the moment until you end up with your bar of choice on that day.

That's not logic, that's emotion.

And that same principal works whether it's a bar of chocolate or a house and everything in between.

Now I know you're sitting there thinking "that's ridiculous" but I can assure you, I've had this conversation hundreds of times in training sessions and emotion wins through every time.

The next thing to think about is how the two go together.

The best way I've found to do it is to link them with the words 'which means'.

Let me show you.

A feature 'which means' a benefit or if you prefer, it does this 'which means' you get this.

For example,

We have them in packs of six 'which means' you'd no

longer be hungry. Very basic I know, but you get the idea.

Let me tell you a little story about logic and emotion.

Picture the scene, we wake up on a Saturday morning and I am reliably informed that we need to go and buy a new fridge.

So I jump out of bed full of excitement (not) and off I go to suffer the joys of traipsing around numerous shops until my will to live just decides to curl up and die.

I can't tell you how many shops we went to or even the name of the one we ended up in, but there we are, stood in front of two almost identical fridges. They are the same size, the same energy rating, the same everything. The only difference is that one is white and one is grey. Oh, and the grey one is about £50 more.

Take a wild guess as to which one we bought?

Yep, you guessed it, the grey one.

Take a guess at why?

I kid you not when I tell you that the reason we bought the grey one is because it matched the colour of the handles on the kitchen cupboards!

There is absolutely no logic in that decision, it is 100% emotion.

I've told this story in many training sessions and every time I do, all the women in the room nod approvingly and all the men have blank looks on their faces.

The moral of the story for features and benefits?

Know and understand the features (logic) of your product/service.

Know and understand the benefits (emotion) of your product/service and which features they match.

The problem comes when you get caught up in telling your customer all the features and not enough of the benefits. I've seen it many times before, people get so caught up in telling people how great their product or service is and forget that the customer doesn't really care about that, they just want to know what's in it for them.

One thing you have to get your head around is that although there may well be a dozen or more benefits to using your product or service, the customer won't necessarily care about all of them – so telling them all of them has no advantage and will just serve to cause them to stop listening to you – the trick is that as you have a conversation with them, in your head you work out which of the benefits you have are most likely to appeal to them and those are the ones that you tell them, and only them.

Let's summarise...

Features are logic, benefits are emotion. People don't buy on logic, they buy on emotion. There will be several benefits to your product/service, but you only talk to the customer about the ones that make sense or benefit them.

And it all works best if you add the words 'which means' between the two.

You don't necessarily have to say the words each time but have it in your head that it's how you join a feature to a benefit.

Chapter Two

3. Open and Closed Questions.

Again, the principal behind this is relatively simple. Closed questions require a simple yes or no answer.

Example: *Is your favourite colour blue?*

Open questions require a fuller answer (and is something that you can usually expand on)

Example: *What's your favourite colour?*

Very simple examples I'll agree but I did say it was relatively simple. The hard part comes with learning how and when to use them.

So let's take a look at that in a bit more detail.

Generally, you want to be using open question through the vast majority of your presentation and only turn to closed questions when you want a yes or no answer.

Open questions are those that allow you to expand on the answer a customer gives you, ideally with another question and therefore building a conversation which is exactly want you want.

What you'll end up with once you have got a bit of practice is that you'll be able to fairly precisely guess at what their answer will be and consequently what your next question will be and so on.

This is how you build that conversation I keep mentioning.

It's called 'building a rapport'. Rapport is one of those things that most people see as mystic art and salespeople see as an absolute necessity. Being able to build a rapport with someone and making it look like you didn't mean to is a skill.

As a trainer of 20 years, I have had to refine this skill. Imagine how effective a training session would be if I didn't make the people in the room feel relaxed and want to listen to me – not so much fun I'm sure.

I know I'm going off track a bit but being able to build rapport is a pretty vital component in a successful sale.

I have been asked hundreds if not thousands of times 'how long does it take to build a rapport?' and I can't answer that. Not because I don't know but because there is no set time, it takes as long as it takes. Not very helpful I know but as I said, there is no set time.

I've seen it so many times when someone has had some training that dictates the amount of time spent on each part and doesn't quite hit the mark.

I hate to burst your bubble, but that's just never going to work. Sales isn't like that, you cannot be that precise with it. In training sessions, I always explain it like this. The people you're speaking to haven't been on this course so they don't know what they're supposed to say and when their supposed to say it. Damned inconvenient I know but that's how it is.

I'll cover some more on this later but for now let's get back to open and closed questions.

Quick summary, you use open questions from the start of you call/meeting/presentation and only turn to closed questions when you want a yes or no answer.

Using a closed question too soon will stop you dead in your tracks.

One of the most common mistakes is using a question like

 "Would that be of interest?"

It's a closed question, if you haven't built any rapport, trust etc that question will get you an emphatic no and then your chances of getting that sale are reduced to a big fat zero.

See how that works, closed question too soon and you're on your way home tail between legs.

Unfortunately, I'm about to muddy the water somewhat and my apologies for this but it's necessary.

You will find that some open questions can be answered with a yes or no but you can still move forward with them.

Let me show you.

Instead of 'would that be of interest?'

We ask 'can you see how that might be a benefit?'

If you get a yes, then your response is to just keep going with more of the same. If you get a no, you simple respond with "Really? I'm surprised, you mentioned that…' and then hit them with something they said earlier that contradicts their answer.

A word of warning, don't be smart arse with the above, nobody wants to be shown up or made to look silly – especially if you're trying to sell to them – just aim it at getting some clarification so that you can respond accordingly.

Remember, across the whole of this, it's about you fixing a problem or filling a need they have. It's not about you and showing them how brilliant you are. They don't care.

Word of warning number two. People don't mind being sold to, they just prefer to be sold to well. We've all been on the receiving end of a terrible sale pitch. I'm sure when some of us first started, we even gave a few but that's why it's called a learning curve.

So, build your rapport with open questions (don't panic we'll talk about rapport building again later) and ask your closed question at the end when you want a one word answer (ideally a yes).

4. Objection Handling

It really astounds me that some salespeople will do everything within their power to avoid having to deal with an objection. I just don't get it.

Look at it this way, objection is another word for question. If the prospective customer has questions, then surely it makes sense to answer them so that they are comfortable with everything and want to buy from you.

Let's understand something, no matter how good your product or service, it will not be perfect for everyone, therefore you are going to get objections.

Every product and service will have several regular objections that you will hear time and time again.

Get over it boys and girls and welcome to sales. If sales

was easy we'd all being doing it and I'd be out of a job.

Anyway, back to objections, there are basically two trains of thought when it comes to handling objections.

Prevention and Preparation – let's take a look at them both

Prevention.

This is where you know what the regular objections are, so you put the answers to them into your pitch. Two things happen here.

1. You make your pitch longer than it needs to be and risk boring the customer before you get to the good bit.

2. You put an objection or thought in their head that wasn't there to begin with but now it is and you've just made your life that much harder and possibly put up a barrier to you getting the sale.

Preparation

This is where you know what the regular objections are going to be and rather than put them into your pitch, you have your responses ready and waiting should you need them and only if you need them.

Which do you think sounds better?

A big old pitch full of things they hadn't thought about or a pitch that when you ask a question it is answered quickly and sensibly.

For me preparation is the best approach, it gives a much

better pitch, you answer any questions (objections) quickly and with professional answers and you've only talked about the things you needed to talk about.

I find it increasingly frustrating that people approach training on this by just giving their salespeople the answers to the standard objections. It involves no thought, it very often sounds like a prepared response and if a prospective customer questions it with something the sales person hasn't been told then it all falls apart. Why would you do that?

Sessions I've delivered to clients, on this topic have always centred around a process to handle objections rather than just stock answers to throw out willy nilly.

That way, if you're given an objection you'll be able to answer it, whatever it is.

There are basically three stages

Stage One – Ask back

By this we don't mean just ask them the same question. What it means is ask them a question which will allow you to establish the grounds of the objection. Very often, especially at the beginning of your pitch, people will use a 'throw away' objection to stop you going any further. What you have to do is understand whether what they've said is a 'throw away' or an actual real objection (question)

For example;

Client "do I have to have insurance …?"

You "It will protect you against …"

This is most likely a fairly standard objection but as I've mentioned, you may find that their initial question isn't the real objection, so by "asking back" we know which way to handle their query.

Stage Two – Empathise

Forgive me if this is a bit obvious but there's a difference between empathy and sympathy. To put it simply, sympathy is 'I feel sorry for you' empathy is 'I understand your situation'. Getting the two mixed up means this won't work.

Empathising with the customer basically means that we agree with their thoughts, the reasoning that lead them towards the objection, rather than agreeing with the objection itself.

For example;

"I can understand your reason for that Mr …… lots of our customers thought the same before joining us" or something similar.

What it does is firstly, show that you understand the concerns they have and secondly, that they're not the first person to have that concern and the others that did got over it and bought from you.

Stage Three – provide the answer

We do this by first establishing the clients needs or concerns (stage one and two) and then matching them with the appropriate benefit.

Remember I said that people buy benefits not features.

So the answer that you give to the objection that they have is always given in the form of a benefit.

If that doesn't satisfy them then you just keep looping round until you give an answer that they are happy with.

I cannot stress this enough, always make sure you don't move forward from this stage until the client is happy.

What happens if you don't I hear you ask?

If you move on from an objection without making sure that they are happy with the answer you gave them, that objection (or concern) will remain unanswered until later and not to put to fine a point on it, will come back and bite you on the bum and very possibly cost you a sale.

Remember, it's not about you, it's about them.

And the proof that it works sits with my Son Jack. He uses the stuff in this book all the time. He has, for example, on more than one occasion, been a tiny bit late with his homework and has therefore had a chat with the teacher and got out of detention.

He has also, from a very young age, understood that we buy on emotion and when approaching me for the "Daddy can I have some money" as all kids do, he would pitch me for it offering a benefit to me giving him money.

I know I'm not supposed to encourage him, but sales skills are life skills and it's a big bad world out there – and I am a Sales Trainer after all so I can hardly complain.

Mind you, this is the same Son that in junior school when his teacher shouted stop to the whole class he responded with 'Hammer time'.

First time I met that teacher she looked at Jack, looked at me and the relationship we have and said "Now I understand".

Chapter Three

5. Closing

Now this is a big one in the sales environment. If you don't or can't close your career in sales is going to be a short and uneventful one.

Even if sales is not your first responsibility and it's something that you have to do to keep things ticking over, if you can't close, your business is going to struggle. Reputation and referrals from friends will only get you so far.

So what is closing?

When I ask that in sales training sessions, I get a variety of answers but one that always comes out is 'Getting the order' or 'Getting the cheque' or something along those lines.

They're not wrong, getting an order would absolutely be a close. Hence the term 'Closing the deal' but for me it starts much sooner than that.

Take it back a few steps, closing is getting agreement from your customer (prospective or otherwise) to move to the next stage. Even if that stage is just arranging to call them back at a certain day and time. It's basically a commitment from both sides to take some action.

Now there are hundreds if not thousands of different closes and my suggestion is that once you find the ones that work for you, stick to them. If them worked once, they'll work again and the more you use them the better you'll get at them and then you'll sound like you've been doing it your whole life!

Let me take you through some of the more popular (and therefore easier) ones, then you can pick the one(s) that you like and get to practicing.

Alternative Close – offering a couple of choices with the intention that they will pick one of the two you offer and you move forward from there.

Assumptive Close – this one takes a bit of practice (and confidence) you basically talk as if they've already decided to buy the product/service from you.

Conditional Close – it goes something like "So if I can get you xxxx they we'll place the order shall we" you link you resolving their objection to them placing an order.

It works really well if you use it to follow up on an alternative close – it also means you will have closed them twice in the same conversation, which is a really good thing.

Price Promise Close – a fairly obvious one, not one I'm very fond of but if you're in a position to price match and cost is the only thing stopping them saying yes, then what the heck, go for it.

Quality Close – sell on quality not price. The best price does not always mean the best product/service.

Think about this for a minute

Price V's Cost

Price is how much you physically pay for something. Cost is what it will cost you to not have it or do it.

When somebody asks you the price, you can respond with "Do you mean the price or the cost?"

Most people will assume that they are the same thing and then you can launch into a short but sweet explanation based on the above, focusing of course on the cost part and throwing in a couple of relevant benefits to add to the fun - which also means that you've just automatically resorted to your objection handling process and of course won the day (or the sale, whichever is more fun)

Yes Close – A yes close is when you get the prospective customer to say yes as many times as possible during your pitch. It doesn't matter what you get them to say yes to, it's just about getting them into a 'yes' frame of mind.

I've had lots of fun with this one over the years. I normally cover closing in the latter part of a sales training day. After each section I'll say something like "Does that make sense" or "Everyone happy with that" basically getting them to say yes lots of times throughout the day.

Then we go through the closing session, I bring up the yes

close and then you see it on their faces as they realise I've been doing it to them all day. It's a bit naughty but it makes the point.

There's something else I learnt right at the start of my career. It's a way to get people to think about what they've said during your conversation and makes them give you reasons why they should buy from you.

Feel free to tweak it to match your own approach but it goes something like this.

Like – Use – Understand – Afford

"So xxxx do you like the xxxx we offer?"

"Yes"

"Great, and do you think you could use it?"

"Yes"

"And do you understand how it works? Basically, have I explained it properly?

"Yes"

"Perfect, so what we're saying is that you **like** the idea, you could **use** it, I explained it properly, so you **understand** it all. So what it's down to is whether or not the price works for you, basically, is it affordable?"

"Yes"

"OK, let's see what we can do with that"

The idea being that if you've built enough value and trust in the conversation you've had with them then they've just told you that the only thing stopping them from buying it is whether or not they can **afford** it.

This is a fun one...

"If it was free would you have it?"

"Yes!"

"If it was £10,000 would you have it?"

"No!"

"OK, so you and I have to find the amount where you stop saying no and start saying yes, sound like a plan?"

Now agreed, all of this stuff is aimed at closing at the end of the conversation and I said you can close at any time - and you can.

Lots of sales teams that I meet have an internal (Telesales) team calling out to make appointments for the field sales team so let's look at their type of close.

Their aim is to get the prospective customer to agree to meet with the someone from the field team, so they're effectively making an appointment – or getting you to agree to give up some of your time.

They would still go through all the stuff we've talked about, the same techniques etc. and then they have to get a date/time pinpointed.

Try this…

"I know he has some free time Wednesday and Thursday next week, do either of those suit you?"

"Thursday would work"

"OK, is morning or afternoon better for you?"

"Afternoons generally"

"OK, 2pm or 4pm?"

"4pm"

"Perfect, we'll see you on Thursday at 4pm" What you have there, as I'm sure you all noticed, was three, yes three, alternative closes. What you've also done by using

this technique is making the prospective customer think that it was their idea because they made the choices for you. I know I made that sound all very easy, so to liven it up a bit, if they say they can't do either of those days, you say,

"That's OK, what day would be good for you?"

They pick a day (hopefully) and you pick up the rest of the process and get the same result.

Let me just clarify one thing before we go any further.

Nobody, and I mean nobody, can close everyone. Even the best salespeople in the world don't close everyone. So if you don't get the sale, don't be discouraged, debrief yourself, work out where you think you missed it, learn from it and get the next one.

There are so many more types of close, but I don't want to completely blow your mind with all of them. Firstly, because you probably won't need most of them and secondly, because closing is only a part of the sales process and to be perfectly honest with you, if you don't get the other stuff right, you won't get the opportunity to close anyway.

As I've said before, let's get the understand basics, the fundamental building blocks if you like. When you can build value and the belief and trust in you is there from the customer side, the closing part becomes so much easier.

So let's not break into cold sweats just yet, this is only the beginning. For now, let's just get to grips with how the whole sales malarky thing works and then we can get into the cool stuff that will really help you stand out and wonder why you ever worried about sales.

6. Follow Up

This quite an important one when you consider that a big part of getting the sale is about building trust. I mentioned trust earlier, it's massively important in sales and to be fair, with life in general. If you don't trust somebody you're not going to be their biggest fan and you're certainly not going to give them your hard earned cash, are you?

So, in terms of following up on a conversation you had with a prospective customer, if you tell them you are going to do something, then make sure that you do it. It doesn't matter how small or insignificant it might seem to you, to them it's a test of your standing in their mind and any future dealings you might have with them.

So follow up on what you said. It doesn't matter if you promised to send an email, call them back or whatever it is. If you said you'd do it, then make sure you do it. It's important to the relationship.

Call backs are a good example of solid follow up. If you agreed to call them back at a certain date/time then do everything in your power to make sure you do it.

I don't care if when you call back at the agreed date/time that they weren't there or they weren't available. The bottom line is that you did what you said you would do.

And I promise you, they'll know.

Even if you have to do these three or four times and you never get to speak to them, it doesn't matter. You're building trust and showing that you can be relied upon.

It works especially well if you're dealing with someone's P.A. because a good P.A. is trusted completely by their boss and if they say you're worth talking to because you've made the effort, then you'll get your chance.

Another quick tip on this is to ask the P.A.'s name, remember it and use it next time you speak to them.

Make it personal and it'll do wonders for you.

They get used to most salespeople seeing them as in the way and therefore treat them as such. By treating them as an equal you stand out.

Follow up on what you said you'd do, I promise you it's worth it.

It's probably worth mentioning the Gatekeeper at this point.

It's another one of those things that untrained salespeople see as a hurdle to get past, as something that's in their way and as such tend to treat them with undeserved contempt.

The Gatekeeper is the person who first answers the phone when you call a business – assuming of course that you don't have the direct line of the person you want to speak to and that it's them that answers the telephone.

With Gatekeepers it's fairly easy, just be firm but polite. Simple.

The thing you have to understand is that the gatekeepers' job is to put calls through – admittedly there's far more to it than that, but this is the bit that concerns us.

This is the sort of approach you want to make.

"Hello, John Smith please"

"Could I ask who's calling please?"

"Of course, it's Nick Jones"

If you're lucky then they'll put you through on the basis of that.

Why? Because you made it sound like you know them and that they would know you, just by the manner in which you approached it.

I said before that you won't be able to sell to everyone and by the same token, this won't work with everyone.

What's likely to happen is they'll add a question like

"Can I ask what it's about?"

Word of warning number three, don't get caught up telling

them too much. You'll launch into a full pitch about how wonderful your product/service is, how you don't understand how they survived without it for so long etc.

And the Gatekeeper will just say to their boss "It's some bloke about xxxx" before coming back to you and saying "No thanks"

The reason that happens is because no Gatekeeper in the world is ever going to say what you said with the same passion that you will, so don't waste your time. Just put together a quick one liner that will catch their interest when it's repeated and get you where you want to be.

There's not much else you can do except that, it's trial and error, it's a hard slog that if you stick to it will work. Remember I said you won't sell to everyone? Well, you won't get past every Gatekeeper either so don't lose sleep over it.

As with the P.A. ask their name and use it next time you call.

I appreciate that we've covered a lot already and forgive me but there's loads more yet. But do not fear, by the time we're done you'll have all the knowledge you need to speak to someone with confidence and passion and not only get more sales than you ever did before but you'll also wonder why you ever worried so much about it.

Chapter Four

Right, next step, let's take what we've done so far and put it all together.

Lots of people argue that what I'm about to show you is old hat and out of date. But obviously I would disagree, otherwise I'm going to look a tad silly showing it to you aren't I?

I get so frustrated with everyone trying to invent new ways and telling everyone to 'Think outside the box'. I just don't get it, what's in the box is perfectly fine, has worked for years and still works. I'm all about getting the fundamentals right and the rest will come with experience.

This process has been around for many, many years. I've taught it to 1000's of salespeople across the globe and it still works. It's simple, easy to remember and it works.

Attention, Interest, Desire, Action.

The model was developed in 1898 by St Elmo Lewis in an attempt to explain how personal selling works. The model laid out a sequence that describes the process a salesperson must lead a potential customer through in order to achieve a sale.

Let's break each one down in turn so you can get to grips with it.

ATTENTION

The first thing you want to do whether it's a sales call, a meeting, a presentation or anything else is to get the attention of your prospect.

On the phone that's going to be with your tone of voice. Firm, polite, professional and to the point – in this instance you've got about 7 to 10 seconds so make them count. It doesn't sound very long but I promise you it's long enough.

Face to Face you do it with a firm handshake and the same tone of voice as above. It will also help if you're dressed accordingly – first impressions count but we'll talk about that later.

INTEREST

The next thing you need to do, now you've got their attention, is to build some interest in you and your product/service.

This is where the features come in (remember those?) this is where you start to talk about the really cool stuff that it does, or you can do for them.

Word of warning number four, don't put too much emphasis on the features, remember people buy on benefits not features. The features are important but they are a building block to the benefits and what they get out of it.

Features are the logical part, it's where you build their level of 'interest' ready to hit them with the benefits and the emotional part, or to stick to the plan, the desire.

DESIRE

This is the fun one. Desire is the emotional part and the part where you can really stand out.

We've already talked about benefits being the emotion and that people buy the benefits of your product/service. So here's how you do it.

The idea here is to get your prospective customer to imagine what it would be like have what you're offering them, to see with 'their minds eye' how much better things would be if they had it. How much more effective or efficient things would be.

You get the idea, you have to make them think "How the heck have we managed so far without it". People buy on emotion, so you therefore have to make them look at what you offer emotionally.

Once you've got it to that point, it's time for the final piece.

ACTION (CLOSE)

You want them to take action, and by that we ideally mean that they buy from you what you want them to buy.

I know that sounds a bit like a 'perfect world' but actually, if you do it all right then you almost don't have to do the last part – the close – because they will already be sold on the idea/product/service and them doing it is a given.

Unfortunately, we don't live in a perfect world and most of the time you'll have to work for it right to the last minute.

But that's why we have been through the basic skills needed so that you can, with confidence, have a 'sales' conversation and close the deal!

Within the INTEREST/DESIRE stages is when you are delivering your pitch and building that rapport.

It's where the important stuff happens but be aware, it's also where you can mess it up and lose the sale forever.

To summarise;

Get their ATTENTION

Highlight the features to gain INTEREST

Build DESIRE but utilising benefits and emotional thinking.

And then finish it all off by closing it all off and getting them to take a ACTION (CLOSE)

You can actually use this same process when you're writing your script. More on scripts later.

When it comes to sales, first impression count. Fact.

When it's face to face and you're meeting a prospective customer for the first time you can generally get a good first impression by dressing accordingly and giving a good handshake.

When it's on the phone, it's all about what you say and how you say it. As I said before, you've got about 7 – 10 seconds to get it right so you need to put some real thought into how you approach it.

As always, I'm going to talk you through it and tell you what you need to know.

Let's focus on face to face first.

If it's a first meeting, smart business attire is normally a good start point. Although the definition of what that is has changed over the years.

When I first started in business it was suit and tie no questions asked.

These days you can rock up in a suit and shirt with no tie and it's reasonably well accepted. The caveat I would add to that is think about who you're going to see and whether or not that's acceptable to them?

For example, if they work in an industry where a suit and tie is the given dress code then you should do the same.

By the same token, if the industry is a little more relaxed then you can be too. But never go too far, this is still a business meeting and you're expecting this person to at some point, part with their money so dress accordingly.

As an example, if you came to a meeting with me in jeans and a T-Shirt, it'll be a very short and somewhat unfruitful meeting for you.

Just put some thought into it folks, it's not rocket science.

Handshakes are another minefield. I was always taught to give firm handshake and look the person in the eye. It's just polite.

We've all had those sweaty, limp handshakes. They're no fun and it gives you entirely the wrong impression that person.

If you're not confident in your handshake, then I suggest you practice it until you are. First impressions count.

Just take some time to think about these things, the details are important folks, the details matter, and you can be damn sure that the people that you're aiming to sell to are looking at every possible angle to say no to you until you build that trust etc. So, give yourself a head start and make some effort.

Now let's look at on the telephone.

I've said it already, on the telephone it is all about what you say and how you say it. Fact.

You have a few seconds to make that first impression, so you have to make them count.

It's about your voice. It's about the words you use and how you deliver them. As always, we'll get into more detail later.

The difficulty you have between the two is that when you walk into someone's office, you can see them and immediately get a judgement on their mood, demeanor etc. On the telephone all you have is the sound of their voice and you have to decide from that whether it's safe to carry on or if you should duck out and live to fight another day – but that's just part of the fun.

We're all painfully aware that making a good first impression is important in many situations.

We also all know that making a bad first impression can absolutely ruin the chance of whatever it was you were trying to do (or impress).

How about this for a question.

Do you think you can recover from a bad first impression?

We've started this debate in many a training session and it's always fairly divided.

Some just give it an outright no. What's done is done. Move on and forget about it.

Others say that with time, yes you can. If you can get past that initial hiccup and offer a great service etc then with time you can probably all laugh about it. But the big 'if' here is you being able to get past the initial bad impression – I guess it all depends on how bad an impression you made!

Of course, the obvious answer is don't put yourself in that position, plan ahead, think about the possible hurdles and make a good first impression.

Let's talk about communication skills and how many of us struggle with understanding them and using them correctly.

We communicate every day, with all sorts of people in all sorts of ways. As I mentioned at the beginning, there are so many more choices in how we communicate then ever before – which means the ways in which we can get it wrong have also increased.

Oddly enough and I guess because of what I do, I'm obviously a fan of straight up conversation either face to face or on the telephone.

People who I've worked with will tell you that after about 3 or 4 emails/text I get bored and pick up the phone.

It's purely my own opinion but I do feel that social media, emails and such like have made salespeople lazy.

I regularly get emails from people I've never met telling me that their business is wonderful, they've done all this stuff and I'm crazy for not using them.

And then ask me to go to a link and select a time in their diary for them to talk to me. I can usually never get to the delete button fast enough!

But any way, back to communication skills.

Professor Albert Mehrabian of UCLA, one of the foremost experts in personal communications, conducted a landmark study to measure the relationship between the three elements that are communicated when we interact with others.

- Verbal – What we say (the words we actually use)

- Vocal – How we say it (pitch, pace, tone etc.)

- Visual – What people see (appearance and body language)

What we're talking about here is when we're out and about on our normal day, nothing precise or specific. Just day to day life.

He found that the greater the degree of inconsistency between the three elements, the less credible the message will be to the recipient.

To achieve credibility with your customers it is vital that there is consistency between what you say and how you say it.

Albert says it splits into three main parts

- Body language

- Tone

- Words

And they look like this...

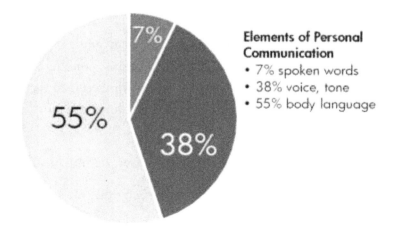

Elements of Personal Communication
- 7% spoken words
- 38% voice, tone
- 55% body language

You can imagine the heated debates we've had when talking about this in training sessions. It's a huge can of worms but it's important to understand it and what it means to you for sales.

Looking at the amount of focus on body language, you can now see why we put so much value behind first impressions. Why that handshake etc are so necessary.

When you're in a face to face sales situation, body language is something that you'll need to pay a bit of attention to as it will help you read the situation and the level of interest your customer has.

The question for you now is does it change when you're on the telephone?

According to most people the answer is a huge yes, of course it does.

Although I would disagree slightly. The general opinion is that it changes to 80% Tone and 20% Words with Body Language being completely out of the picture.

For me, although I would agree that you can't see body language when someone is on the telephone, having trained 1000's of people who work entirely on the telephone, I can assure you that their body language can and will affect their tone of voice.

Chapter Five

On the subject of tone of voice, let's dig a bit deeper on that for a minute.

Remember I said that on the telephone it's all about what you say and how you say it.

Used properly, the voice is a wonderful tool that can get you all sorts of things, depending on how you use it.

The voice can be broken down into five controllable parts. Pitch, Pace, Volume, Articulation and Energy.

The correct or as important, incorrect use of each of them can give the same sentence an entirely different meaning or to put it another way, the perception of it can.

Let me explain,

Pitch – if the pitch of your voice is quite high then the person you're speaking to will make an assumption as to the type of person you are. The same goes for if the pitch of your voice is quite deep.

People will judge you on it. I'm by no means saying that it's the right thing to do, what I'm saying is that they're going to do it so take in into consideration.

Pace – Pace is important in sales, if you talk too fast people will think 'what's he trying to hide, why is he rushing'. If you talk to slowly, their assumption is that you're not sure what you're doing, and they will therefore lack confidence in you.

Volume – if you're too loud, they think 'why are they shouting at me' as they hold the phone three foot from their ear.

If you're volume is too low, as in you're too quiet. They'll got bored of straining to hear you very quickly and the call will be cut short.

Articulation – always a good one. If you over articulate people can feel patronised which is never going to go in your favour. And as before, they will make an assumption as to the type of person you are.

Conversely, if you are borderline talking in slang and can't put together a decent sentence, then you will be in trouble.

Remember also that I said people don't mind being sold to, they just prefer to be sold to well and the way you speak to them is a big part of that, whether it's face to face or over the telephone.

Last but by no means least, energy.

Energy is an interesting one. As a salesperson, you're expected to be passionate about what you're selling but there's a fine line.

Being too energetic will cause people to back away and

wonder how much Red Bull you put on your cereal.

Going the other way and not being energetic enough about it at all will make them think 'if it doesn't excite you then why on earth would I buy it from you'.

I'm not saying you should entirely change your voice for selling. What I'm saying is that you need to be aware of how you sound, how your voice comes across and the perception of the person you're speaking to.

We can, of course, break it down even further.

Pauses – pauses are much like pace. Too many pauses and they're unsure if you know what you're talking about – and therefore your credibility will take a hit.

No pauses at all and you seem like you're rushing. Again, not great for the credibility, because all they're thinking is 'what are they hiding'.

Inflections – you can actually have a bit of fun with these. Inflections are the words that you emphasise to make them stand out.

If you look back at the closing stuff we talked about, you'll see how using inflection can really make something sound appealing and something they'd be a fool not do do.

The last one I'm going to pick up on is Verbal Repetitions.

Ever heard two teenage girls have a conversation when they throw the word 'like' in every few words?

That's Verbal Repetition.

That's not too bad I hear you say. But here's the downside. If someone has a Verbal Repetition, what happens is that, in a sales conversation, if you have a Verbal Repetition, the person you're speaking to starts listening out for the repetition and not everything else you're saying.

See the problem?

There are all kinds of different ones, like people saying 'OK too many times or 'Um' is another good one.

It doesn't really matter what it is, if you have one, do your best to kerb it.

Just to reiterate what I said earlier, I'm not saying you should entirely change your voice for selling, that's not sustainable. What I'm saying is that you need to be aware of how you sound, how your voice comes across and the perception of the person you're speaking to.

To be sensible, we should probably mention listening skills as a follow on from communication.

Quick question, what is the difference between listening and hearing.

Hearing is something you do as standard. Unless you put your fingers in your ear, you are going to hear what's going on around you regardless of whether you want to or not.

Listening is a conscious choice. You choose to listen.

Active listening is a great skill for someone in sales to be good at. Nobody likes to be interrupted when they're talking, it's rude for a start.

In its most basic form Active Listening is doing things like nodding when someone is talking to you. Asking questions of them, looking them in the eye and so on.

That's also the stuff you should be looking out for if you're the one doing the talking.

On the telephone it's slightly different. You're listening for responses to what you're saying. If you think you've lost them, ask a question.

You'll have to pay more attention when you're on the phone because there will obviously not be any body language to pick up on.

Before we go on, I'm going to throw a bit of a tip sheet in to cover off what we've covered so far.

Enjoy what you're doing...

If you enjoy what you're doing, firstly, it won't seem like such hard work and secondly, the customer will hear it in your voice and therefore is more likely to respond positively. There are worse things you could be doing that having a nice little chat with someone about how fab you are your business are. So just go with it and have some fun.

People buy people first...

Human nature dictates that people "buy" from people they like. Your aim is to conduct yourself in such a way that the customer is comfortable with you and what you're telling them.

Think about this, unless your life depended on it, would you buy from somebody you didn't like?

It's not a 100% but it's fairly unlikely. So be polite, be nice, be professional and know what you're talking about.

Features and Benefits...

We went over this quite a lot. When people "buy"
something they want to know what's in it for them. Use
the features and benefits of the product to help the
customer make the decision to buy. But remember, focus
on the benefits that matter to them, not the ones you think
will work. Everyone is different, so have the conversation
and work it out from there.

Smile while you dial...

Obviously more of a telephone thing and although I
appreciate that it sounds a bit cheesy, but if you're cheery,
chatty and literally smile down the phone, it does and will

make a difference to how you sound and the perception the customer has of you.

I'm by no means suggesting that you sleep with a coat hanger in your mouth, just smile.

Be a good listener…

Another old school, cheesy quote for you but it makes sense. We have two ears and one mouth we should use them to that ratio. Listen to what the customer says, it will give you all the information you need (and probably some you don't!!) and it's the best way to find out what the client actually wants/needs.

Paint word pictures…

Build a picture in their mind, create enough interest and desire with what you say so that the customer wants the product/service. This is that part in the conversation were you're pulling out all the benefits and the sexy stuff and really building that desire part up.

Use product names…

It will give you credibility and make the customer feel safe and trust you. It shows them that you understand their industry and can talk to them on a level playing field. Nothing worse than someone selling to you that doesn't really know what they're doing or talking about.

Make sure you use full names not jargon - unless you are selling into a jargon based industry, like IT for example.

Control the conversation…

I know that sounds a bit ominous, but it's important. I've seen and heard too many sales be lost because there was no control and it all just petered out or they forgot to ask for the business/sale.

Lead the conversation to where you want it to go by using open/closed questions and by utilising features and benefits. Just like we talked about.

Build Rapport.

I said I'd talk more about this so here goes.

Building a rapport is not something that you can put a time limit on or expect to just happen. It takes time and effort. You can't rush it and you can fake it.

I've seen/heard some interesting attempts at this over the years, some of them were quite painful to listen to.

It all boils down to this. Find some common ground, have a good conversation, ask questions, listen and you will find the way.

It's like riding a bike and not putting any oil on the chain.

It's still going to work but it's going to be tough going and if you're not careful something might break.

The problem for most people is that when they get into a sales situation, they start talking in ways they wouldn't normally, or they feel awkward and struggle with it.

Remember what I said earlier,

"Ponder on this for a moment, if I asked you to talk to

someone and explain to them what it is that you do, you could undoubtedly keep that going for a while and not be overly concerned.

Now try it this way, talk to someone and explain to them what you do and then ask them to pay you to do it"

And this is usually where the rapport building falls apart. We panic, we know we're supposed to do it, but we don't do it naturally and that's when it becomes painful.

So deep breath, focus and just have a conversation.

Chapter Six

If you've ever read anything about Nero Linguistic Programming or the like, then you'll be aware that the mind is a wonderful thing but it can also be somewhat bent to your will if you know what you're doing.

I appreciate that that sounded a bit on the supernatural side and like I'm about to show you a technique to hypnotise your prospective customer into buying from you.

But I'm not.

What I'm talking about is phrases and wording that you can use, at specific points to encourage a positive result.

It's about reading people, understanding their reactions to certain things and responding accordingly.

We've all heard about the 'power of suggestion', well that's all it is.

Go back to the chapter on closing and look at the 'Yes' close. What you're doing the whole time you are delivering that yes close is the power of suggestion. You are getting people used to saying yes as if it was the most natural thing to say.

In fact, look at closing in it's entirety.

Pretty much any close you do is using the power of suggestion to some degree, however small.

But it starts way before that. Within the whole conversation you are going to have with your prospective customer you are going to use certain words and phrases to not only lead the conversation but to get the customer into a position that they trust you and can see how your product/service will benefit them.

It goes back to what I said about building the desire, about painting word pictures. It's about getting your customer to really think what it would be like if they actually had your product/service. How they've somehow managed so far but now they wouldn't have to.

It's like when Nicola says to me "Do you want to cook dinner tonight?"

What she actually means is "You're cooking dinner tonight"

But by saying it the way she does, I don't feel like I'm being told what to do (we all know how much us men like that) and I usually respond with "Yeah OK" like it was my idea!

See how that works?

I'll give you another example.

I worked for a water softener company a few years ago. I actually ran the telesales team. The team were tasked with booking appointments for the techs to go and demonstrate the system.

One of the questions they asked was,

"Are you interested in the quality of your water?"

Most people the team spoke to said they weren't because it's a fairly ordinary question.

So we changed it to "Are you concerned about the quality of your water?"

We just changed a couple of words, but it gave an entirely different feel to the question.

Now suddenly, people were saying "No I'm not, should I be?"

Now let me be very clear, the team did not then burst into a hundred reasons why they should be concerned, they just suggested that checking it out might be useful.

But it makes my point, wording something in the right

way gives an entirely different feel to it.

Just to be really clear, I'm not for one second suggesting that you start making stuff up or outright lying to people. What I'm saying is that if you word things properly, you'll get a better response.

Ask yourself a question. Do you remember everything about your day, your afternoon, even your last meeting?

In most cases, the answer is "no, not really".

As an example, I used to call my Mum every Sunday, 6 pm without fail. The only time I didn't would be if I was actually with her on a Sunday.

Now when I called, we'd talk about all sorts of things, sometimes just for 20 minutes and other times for an hour depending on how busy a week we'd both had.

I can assure you, if you called her an hour after we'd spoken and asked her what we talked about, she'd probably be able to remember about half of it if we're lucky.

This is very normal and the case for a very high percentage of us as we all lead busy lives and don't always choose to recall everything.

So if my own Mother is going to struggle, what chance have I got with a prospective customer I've never met before?

This can actually be used to your advantage if we use

influencing.

One of the easiest and quickest ways to help influence others is to give a small number of options, providing your favoured option at the end.

So an estate agent might say something like "Would you like to buy the one bedroom or the two bedroom?"

Said with good eye contact and a gentle nod of the head as you say, *"two bedroom"*, the respondent will naturally favour the last option. This will be the first thing they will remember and importantly, that they see subconsciously, you nodded approval for that option (obviously on the phone we use inflection in our voice rather than nodding!)

To further nudge it in your favour, you can add a "what's in it for me" such as...

"Would you like to buy the one bedroom or the two bedroom? The two beds have far better views".

You can use this when influencing as a way of persuading customers down a certain path or process.

The other thing to add into this is something called 'Last Heard, First Remembered'

It basically means that the thing that you want the customer to remember the most is the last thing you say to them.

If we use agreeing to an appointment as an example, you would say.

"OK, that's all booked in for you. We'll look forward to seeing you on Tuesday at 2:00 pm"

So that whatever else may have been talked about in that conversation, the last thing they heard (and consequently the first thing they'll remember) is their appointment.

We could go on for pages with this but I'm sure you get the idea. It's about using positive words, using the benefits and just listening to the customers' needs.

On the topic of customer needs, let's get a bit technical and look at Maslows Hierarchy of Needs

It goes something like this, when you speak to customers, they will have some basic needs in mind. The very least they expect if you like. Your job is to take it further.

When you understand the needs, wants and desires of your customers (and more importantly the differences between them) you are in a position to provide them with the appropriate level of service.

If you think it through, you can improve service and secure their loyalty *and* improve the quality of your interaction with them.

- "Needs" are fundamental expectations, which set the minimum level of required performance. They can be rational (objective functional requirements) or emotional (deeper, more implied needs such as the implications of a brand)

- "Wants" are considered more when needs have been addressed. Meeting them leaves customers happy and satisfied.

- "Desires" can be thought of a 'latent expectations. They are the extras which set some services apart from others. Repeated over time they become "wants". In this way you 'raise the bar' on expectations.

"Our study concludes that this is the percentage of our customers who will buy from us without any effort whatsoever on our part."

What it means is if you understand how it works, you can provide your customers with a product/service that goes beyond what they expected and will secure you that first sale and fingers crossed, many more afterwards.

Just be careful not to take your eye off the ball. Do you

want happy customers or do you want satisfied customers?

As the saying goes "Under Promise, Over Deliver"

There's lots of different approaches to selling, different methods you can use and it's a bit of trial and error to find the one that you're comfortable with.

As we've already talked about, asking the right questions at the right time is fairly important in terms of how successful you might be. One of the most popular methods was written by a chap called Neil Rackham in 1988 and is called SPIN Selling. So I thought I'd put it in here, just for good measure.

SPIN Selling was developed following the observation, by sales experts, of 35,000 sales calls.

Through this observation it became clear that the quality of questions asked by a salesperson were key to the success of a sale. The right questions could speed up the process, whereas the wrong questions could stall it or even halt it completely – remember what I said about using a closed question too soon.

The term **SPIN** is an acronym of four different types of sales questions designed to bring a prospect into interest and through to a sale:

- **SITUATION** questions
- **PROBLEM** questions

- **IMPLICATION** questions

- **NEED/PAY OFF** questions

Situation Questions

The answers to Situation questions form the foundation of a sales cycle. The aim of these questions is to develop an understanding of the prospect and their precise situation (hence the name) in terms of the product/service you offer.

Examples of Situation questions for a selling a CRM system.

- How do you currently manage your customer's contact details?

- How do you keep track of what's happening in your sales pipeline?

- How do you maintain an overview of how your individual sales reps are performing?

The answers you get from these questions is used throughout the remainder of the sales cycle and your conversation.

Of course, the more research you do prior to the initial conversation, the more intelligent and precise your questions will be—and the more useful data you will gather.

Problem Questions

The idea behind Problem questions is to bring the prospect into an awareness that there is a problem or problems that need to be solved. These problems and issues are what you will gently but firmly use to steer them towards a sale - remember 'control the conversation'.

Problem questions are also effective at causing a prospect to identify issues that might have been otherwise overlooked. We've all been in the situation where because things are working OK, we don't really notice an issue or and inefficiency.

Examples of Problem questions:

- Was the amount of training you needed to get up and running with your CRM ever a problem?

- Do you find it's expensive adding new users to your CRM?

- What's the biggest problem you're facing so far when managing your sales pipeline?

Implication Questions

Implication questions are designed to shine a light on the potential impact if the problems and issues named in the Problem questions are not addressed.

Correctly phrased and asked, Implication questions clearly demonstrate to the prospect in their own mind that the problems really need to be solved, sooner rather than later.

Examples of Implication questions:

- If leads don't get input into your CRM system, what's the impact on your sales pipeline?

- If training on your CRM is costly and time-consuming, what does that mean for new reps when they start?

- If you can't accurately see your performance to date, how much response time do you have to implement a fix if you anticipate your sales are falling short of target?

Need/Pay Off Questions

Now that you've brought your prospect to the realisation of how the situation will only deteriorate if it isn't solved, you then want to get them considering how valuable a real solution to the problem or problems would be. That is the point of the Need/Pay Off questions.

Examples of Need/Pay Off questions:

- Why is being able to have a big picture overview of your sales pipeline important to you?

- If you could cut the amount of time spent training new staff on your CRM, what impact would that have?

- If you could see the opportunities in your pipeline at a glance, how would that help you achieve your sales targets?

The secret to getting results with Need/Pay Off questions is to ensure the prospect specifies the benefits themselves. Encourage them to visualize, and imagine the difference with that problem solved - remember, 'paint word pictures' etc.

The beauty of these questions is that if you get them right, your customer will tell you how your product will help.

Need/Pay Off questions need to evoke positive emotions. After all, it feels good to know that an ongoing problem can finally be solved doesn't it.

And if you're the one who has solved it for them, firstly they now think you're fabulous and secondly, they're likely to tell other people thus making a sale to that person a little easier because you were recommended by someone they know and trust so it goes that they will like and trust you initially – just don't mess it up.

That, boys and girls, is called a referral and they are one of if not the best type of lead you can get, so we love them.

Chapter Seven

Let's just take quick breather and look at something a little less intense.

Scripts.

For me they are something that you use to get some kind of structure to the conversation you want to have but as soon as you are able, you should put it to one side and not rely on it too much.

When we train salespeople, we put together a script so that we can practice and get proficient at delivering it but the aim is always for them to be able to go through it without looking at it as quickly as they can.

There's a reason actors practice and then memorise their lines.

Firstly, because they'd look a bit daft on screen or stage if they kept constantly referring to a piece of paper.

Secondly, because it looks and sounds much more natural if you can just say what you need to say. It's more conversational, it's more credible and it's much easier for you to react when the customer asks a question.

If you're on the telephone you can have a sheet of bullet points to hand just in case.

If you're face to face and using a presentation, then ideally that will be enough of a prompt for you to keep going and not miss your step.

As I mentioned earlier, you can use AIDA to structure your script, but the aim is to keep it conversational.

You'll also need to keep account of all the other bits we've gone through.

If you want to be successful in sales, whether it's your main role or something you have to do to keep the business ticking over it requires the right mindset.

If sales are what you do then it's a little easier because you'll be doing it every day so you can build up the skills you need over time and with practice.

If, like a lot of people, it's something that you have to turn your hand to to keep the business going and new customers coming in then you probably need to put some time aside so that you can prepare and focus on it.

Ducking in and out of it will do you no good at all. If at all possible, I would suggest that you put a day or two each week specifically for sales activity. Or if your workload doesn't allow that, maybe just decide to do it a couple of afternoons, you get the idea.

You may well start the process (sales cycle) on the telephone but at some point, you're likely to have to be face to face with a customer.

So think about this,

Be Presentable, we've already talked about first impressions so I'm sure I don't need to tell you what presentable looks like.

Be knowledgeable, this is massively important to both you and the customer. Being knowledgeable about your product/service is paramount. You have to be able to answer any question that the customer throws at you.

If you can't, your credibility goes and we talked about what happens if you don't have that.

Be confident, this links to being knowledgeable. Before you can convince others, you have to be able to convince yourself.

Make sure you fully understand and believe in what you're discussing. It's about how you portray your confidence and body language.

Be proactive, it's easy to become lazy in a sales role. As much as I'm not a fan of the phrase, sales can be a numbers game. The more people you speak to the more your chances increase and the more skillful you become.

Prepare for any meetings you have to go to, do your research, make sure you've got business cards with you.

Check the time of the meeting, aim to be early. There's nothing more likely to blow a sale for you than rocking up late and unprepared.

Agreed, sometimes it's unavoidable but if that's the case, just phone them and tell them. Most people are understanding enough and the same thing has happened to most of us.

I remember one occasion when I was on my way up the M5 to go and meet a prospective new client and I had, what the nice man from the RAC described as a freak accident.

Basically, I had my two passenger tyres side blow out immediately one after the other.

The ironic thing was, the client I was going to see was an accident management company!

I've had some journeys over the years but the only thing you can do is adapt.

I'm a tiny bit of a control freak so when it's in this country, I tend to drive. I don't care if it means getting up at silly o'clock. In my head, if I'm driving, I at least have some semblance of control over the situation.

I remember a drive when I left the clients in Bradford at exactly 6:00 pm and got back to Clevedon at 1:00 am. In case your geography is failing you for the moment, that should have taken about four hours at best but actually took me seven.

One small piece of advice, if you're running late, let the customer know. Then stop round the corner, take an extra couple of minutes to get yourself together and then go in. It's absolutely worth it so you can refocus and give them your best.

In terms of the meeting, have an agenda, at least in your own mind. Know what you want to cover in the meeting. Keep an eye on the customers body language, listen to their tone of voice.

Remember the 'two ears one mouth' phrase. It basically relates to the fact that, certainly in the first meeting, the customer should be talking twice as much as you are.

Remember to listen, it is most definitely going to help you achieve your goal of gaining them as a customer.

Always remember to close.

I know that might sound a bit obvious after all we've talked about, but you'd be surprised how many people have left a meeting and then suddenly gone 'Bugger' and realised they left without any kind of agreed action.

It's the absolute aim of any sales conversation – to get a close.

Now remember what I said about closing. It's not necessarily about getting an order in the first stages. It depends on several things, not least how much it costs.

But always remember that you never finish/leave a sales meeting without some kind of agreed action between you and the customer.

And remember to follow up.

As I've said to probably thousands of salespeople across the globe. Sales is a game and once you know the rules, the game becomes much easier.

The funny part comes when you are faced with a prospective customer who either works in sales or has had some sales training or read a book on sales or watched 'Wolf of Wall Street'.

Don't laugh, I actually had someone say that to me in a training session. My response was to say "OK, sell me this pen"

©Marty Bucella

"If you're not interested in selling your soul, do you mind if I put you on our mailing list?"

People who fit into that category will want to show their dominance. They will want to show you who's in charge.

Quite frankly, I love those meetings.

Firstly, because it's likely to test me a bit which is always good.

And secondly, because I'm a Sales Trainer, if you were as good as you're trying to convince me you are, then we wouldn't be having this conversation.

And as a side note. Salespeople are the best people to sell to because if you do it right, they'll convince themselves for you.

Something else I love with sales team is that frame of mind they get into when December kicks in and they convince themselves that nobody wants to buy.

My answer is always going to be "Are you kidding? In December buying is all they're doing!"

At that time of year people are in a buying mood. It might be for Christmas presents but they're still in a buying mood, So go with it and break the monotony for them with a conversation that doesn't revolve around the festivities.

Goals and targets and the like are always brought into any conversation about sales. That's hardly a surprise but what you do with them and how best to set them is a personal thing and shouldn't be taken lightly.

If you're going to be conducting any kind of sales activity, even if it's just a couple of days a week, then you need to think about this stuff.

As a starting point, let's separate the two.

Goals are the things you want to achieve, targets are the vehicle by which you reach them.

For example, if your goal is to get more sales/customers then you would set yourself a target per week/month etc to get you there.

But let's be sensible, if you're pretty new to sales or it's not really your thing then don't go setting yourself a ridiculous target and consequently setting yourself up to fail. It just defeats the object, leaves you fed up and deflated and gets nobody anywhere.

Start small and build up.

You can also do things like set your target, write it down and change it every time you get a sale.

Word of warning number five, when you do this write the end result down somewhere you can see it and each time you get a sale, reduce the number.

It's a psychological thing, seeing the number reduce is much more enlightening that seeing it go up each time.

So to reiterate, and as an example.

Your goal is to get more sales/customers and your target it to get three more each week.

Reminder time,

Preparation is key. Think about the result from the call you're going to make or the meeting you're going to attend.

Think about how you're going to approach it.

Think about the responses you're likely to get.

Don't assume that the person you're about to speak to knows exactly what you do or understands how it may help them.

Use open and closed questions. There's a difference between the two and they get used at different times.

Open questions are the type of questions that can lead to another question and therefore encourage a conversation.

Closed questions generally only require a yes or no answer and if asked at the wrong time can stop you dead in your tracks.

Features and Benefits

Features are the things that your product/service do for your customers.

Benefits are that they actually care about – nobody buys on the features, they buy on the benefits.

They buy on the 'What's in it for me?'

Think of it like this. Buying is an emotional process, so

when you think of how a feature links to a benefit, remember this…

A Feature 'which means' a Benefit.

Objection Handling

Think in terms of preparation rather than prevention.

Remember that there are three stages to handling and objection.

1. Clarify the questions

2. Empathise

3. Provide the answer

Just remember not to move on until the customer is happy with your answer.

Gatekeepers are part of the process so be nice to them, they're just doing their job.

Closing isn't just about getting the deal, it's about gaining commitment from the customer to move to the next stage – which at some point will be the sale.

Find a close that works for you and keep practising – Alternative, Conditional, Yes, Assumptive and the list goes on.

When you speak to a customer, prospective or otherwise, you need to make sure you deliver a confident and relevant pitch so remember Action, Interest, Desire, Action.

Remember what Professor Albert said about communication.

55% Body Language

38% Tone of Voice

7% Words.

Whether it's face to face or over the telephone, think about your voice and the perception it's giving to the customer. Keep it steady and natural and you won't go far wrong.

Don't push too hard – nobody responds well to pushy salespeople.

Think about how you like to be sold to – if it worked on you then it'll work on others.

Think about what you did to get the customers you already have – if it worked once then it's likely to work again.

Don't assume that the customer knows or understands what you do – that up to you to make clear.

And lastly, don't talk at them, talk to them – have a conversation that you're both involved in.

Chapter Eight

That last line is a good one, don't talk at them, talk to them.

Let me just let thank sink in for a moment.

Don't talk at them, talk to them.

If you are the one being sold to, the last thing you want is for some full on salesperson to launch into the pitch with not even a by your leave.

No chance for you to ask questions or quite frankly, take in most of what they're saying. It's a mistake made by many a person trying to get a sale. They get so caught up in getting everything said and telling you all the features and so on.

Doesn't really work for either side.

When you're delivering your pitch keep these two things in the back of your mind.

1. You are giving a performance not just reciting some words. Be passionate and confident.

2. You're there to have a conversation, so talk to them, ask questions, and listen.

With these in your mind you are likely to get so much

further in the process and your chances of success are much increased.

I've mentioned a couple of times that there are far more channels available to salespeople now than there ever were and as a Sales Trainer I frequently get asked "what's the best sales cycle" or "How do I write my sales process?" and such like.

The answer, regrettably, is not an easy one as there is no "one size fits all" process or cycle for successful sales. There are some standard pieces that should be involved but the thing we have to realise is that every business is different and therefore so are their customers.

There are lots of ways to "make a sale" and you have to find out what works for you. Just remember that it's about the customer and not you, so just because you like the idea is doesn't necessarily mean that everyone will.

One thing I have seen used really well in recent times is adding video into the mix.

We looked at buying a new car a while ago and a week after visiting the showroom, the sales guy sent us a video asking if we'd enjoyed our visit, what we liked about the car most and so on, all whilst sat at his desk with the car we'd looked at perfectly placed over his left shoulder.

Very subtle, but we both noticed it and we both smiled at it.

They say that it can take between 6 and 9 touch points before someone buys from you, especially in todays' world were information is available at the touch of a button.

Touch points don't have to be you actually speaking to someone. They can be an email, them looking at your website, anything really. It's just about keeping you in their mind once you've got there.

Much of your sales process can actually happen without you even knowing.

People are introduced to you and the first thing they do is check you out on LinkedIn.

We talked before about following up on meetings and conversations and adding video to your email signature is really easy to do and is a great way of pushing the message home without being too obvious.

A word of warning at this point, just because your teenage Son says "I post on YouTube all the time" this is your business we're talking about and you can only make a first impression once, so ask someone who knows what they're doing to film it for you. A little money spent at the beginning is money well spent.

Think about how many times you've watch a quick promo video on a website compared to how many times you've scrolled through every page.

In a video you can also use quite a lot of the techniques etc that we've been through in this book.

To return to the question, the best sales cycle or process for you is the one that works best for your business.

Embrace the new ways of selling – New technology, differing work preferences, better business intelligence, alternative communication channels.

There's no point trying to fight it, it's here to stay so welcome it with open arms.

Sales success in today's business climate comes from not just knowing how to sell but also with knowing which medium to use when selling, by knowing how people want to be sold to and what gets them involved in the process.

How we sell has changed, as has the people we are selling to. They generally want things quicker, faster and more immediate. We live in a convenience culture where almost everything is at our fingertips. Making our sales process and activity fit with that is paramount. Gone is the old, accepted way of selling.

It just won't work to any usable degree anymore.

But if you put in place and use the things I've taught you and you're consistent in your delivery then success in sales will come your way.

What is in this book has been working for years and it will continue to work for years because human nature hasn't changed.

Our opinions may change, new things will come along and leave again. People talk about being 'outside the box' etc and you know my opinion about that.

Sales is really quite simple, if you can master the basics then you won't go far wrong. You may have to adapt to changes as they come along but they will just add to your skill.

Once you've mastered the basics you can further improve your chances of success by remembering a few things.

The challenge for you is to not only understand your prospective customers needs but to be able to show them that what you have to offer is going to fulfil those needs (remember we talked about pain points)

And let's not kid ourselves, it is a challenge to get that to happen and to get it to happen regularly but if you take on what we've been through in this book, you should muddle through quite nicely.

Consider the task at hand and approach it properly – if you make a halfhearted approach then you'll get a halfhearted result, and we don't want that do we.

Plan your approach and do the groundwork. Know who you are going to be talking to, find out as much as you can about the business. If you don't know already, take an educated guess at what problems (pain points) they might be facing and tailor your approach (pitch) to fit that.

Understand their needs, you are after all trying to fulfil those needs so it makes sense that you know what they are.

Be professional, we talked about first impressions and everything else that went with it, so I'll say it again, be professional.

Nobody wants or is likely to do business with someone that they don't think is professional. It may not seem very important but I can promise you that it is. No matter what happens, always remain professional. It will, without doubt, benefit you in the long run.

The level to which professionalism is perceived can be largely dependent on the industry you are working in.

They're all different so just be aware – compare a solicitors' expectations and that of say someone in the media industry and you'll see what I mean.

We've talked about asking the right questions at the right time and how that works – and can go horribly wrong if you're not paying attention.

With that in mind, there's a quote by Rudyard Kipling that sums it up quite nicely.

"I keep six honest serving men, they taught me all I knew.

Their names are What and Why and When and How and Where and who"

It's actually part of a longer poem and those that know me will no doubt agree that I'm no poetry connoisseur, but the quote sums up the need for proper questioning rather well.

Going back to open questions, those six words will put you in rather good stead if you use them to find out what you need to know.

OK, next lesson

Value and Urgency.

When you are talking to a prospective customer in a sales

situation, whether it's for the very first time or not,

something you need to do is to create 'value' in what you are offering and give them a sense of 'urgency' about it.

Let's be honest with each other, if they see no value in what you're talking to them about, why on earth would they buy it?

Look at it like this, remember the fridge buying episode I told you about? The salesperson didn't really need to convince us of value because we'd already decided that we wanted one, so we'd covered the value ourselves.

If you are pitching someone about your wonderful product or service, then they might not straight away understand or appreciate the value of it. Therefore, it's your job to show them.

Now be careful when you're doing this because value is a perception and yours might be different than theirs.

As I've said before, don't assume that the person you're speaking to understands what you're talking about, how it would benefit them or can see why it's to their advantage to buy it.

What you say and how you say it (sound familiar?) is what will influence their decision. It's about you getting excited about it, it's about them feeling that excitement and joining in.

Your job is to not only explain it in a way that makes sense to them, but also to show them why it would benefit them to have the product or service.

Therefore, showing VALUE.

Creating a sense of urgency is something different.

To create a sense of urgency with your customer, you basically have to give them the frame of mind that now is the time to buy from you.

Take a look back at the price verses cost analogy that I showed you. Price would absolutely come under value whereas cost fits very firmly under urgency.

Therefore, the urgency is dictated by the cost of you not doing/having it now.

Let me simplify a bit further. Look back at the appointment setting scenario we did. Setting it up in the way that we did, using an alternative close, gives urgency.

We're so busy that we can only offer you two days from next week (subconsciously they now think that you're so busy because everyone wants to see you, therefore you must be great)

It will be different for everyone, but the trick is, as we already agreed, to work out their pain points and show them how your product/service fixes them.

And the sooner they commit to buying your product or service, then the sooner the pain point is gone and life returns to normal.

And that's one of the keys to getting a successful sale. Making their life easier, more efficient, more cost effective and so on is what you're trying to achieve. Or I should say, what you are trying to show them that you can achieve for them.

We've gone through a bunch of stuff in this book and talked about all manner of newfangled techniques that you're supposed to learn so I can imagine that by now your head is spinning and you're wondering where do I start and how the heck to I remember it all and which bit comes first and a million other questions!

My advice is pure and simple. Do not worry!

Becoming good at something takes time and effort and does not happen overnight.

Think about what you do for a job. We're you an expert when you first started. Of course you weren't, you had to learn and practice and make mistakes and that's how you got to be good.

You weren't brilliant overnight, and the same thing applies to you as a salesperson. Take the information in this book, play around with it, practice, find out what works for you.

It's like anything else, you have to build up to it and when you do you can really start to have some fun.

I said it before, sales skills are life skills.

Here's what you do.

1. Take a deep breath.

There's a reason that this book doesn't have hundreds of pages of technical this that and the other. Firstly, because that would be pointless and secondly because that's not how I teach people.

It doesn't work and it doesn't help.

As anyone who has ever been trained or coached by me will tell you, I use stories to make my point. You might not remember the exact words I used, but if you can repeat the story I told you then it'll soon kick in and then the light goes on.

2. You have a copy of this book, so go back to it whenever you need to, make notes on the pages, read it again until it makes sense.

3. You know your product or service better than anyone, so that's not an issue. All you have to do is remember the main points we've talked about and have a conversation with your customer.

4. Don't ever worry or stop mid pitch if you go wrong. Chances are that the customer doesn't know that you did it so just style it out and carry on – in true sales fashion.

What you're aiming for, the end result if you like, it's what's called the Four Levels of Learning.

They work like this,

Level 1 – Unconscious Incompetence

You don't know that you don't know how to do something.

Level 2 – Conscious Incompetence

You know that you don't know how to do something, and it bothers you.

Level 3 – Conscious Competence

You know that you know how to do something, and it takes effort.

Level 4 – Unconscious Competence

You know how to do something, and it has become second nature, you're basically fab at it.

All sounds very deep and meaningful I know so let me give you the analogy that I always use.

Take yourself back to your first ever driving lesson, when you pretty much had no idea whatsoever what you were doing, no clue, zilch, nada didn't even know where to put the key.

That's Unconscious Incompetence.

Then you start to learn a bit but you still don't really know what's going on and it's somewhat frustrating.

That's Conscious Incompetence

Then you have some lessons, and you start to drive around

and change gear and all that fancy stuff but you're still thinking about what to do next.

Now we're at Conscious Competence, you can do it but you have to think about it.

Then you pass your test, and you drive for a while, getting a feel for it, you try some motorways and so on.

Then someone asks you how many sets of traffic lights you went through on the way to work, and you can't answer them.

Not because you weren't paying attention but because driving has become such a natural act that you don't really think about what you need to do, you just do it.

That folks is Unconscious Competence and this is where we want to be.

It's just something that you do. And it's the same state that you're in when you do your job for a few years and it's where you want to aim for in your sales conversations.

If you think about what you're supposed to say next, you won't sound natural.

Much like anything else, it takes time and practice and knowledge.

Well in your hands you now have the knowledge. All you need to do is put in the time and the practice and one day soon it will feel like driving a car.

We've gone through a lot of do that and don't do that in this book, but I just wanted to through in a few more things that people do that will lose them a sale, just for good measure.

It's always helpful to make sure that the person you're about to pitch has time to listen. If they don't and you burst into your presentation, they'll either cut you short or won't really be listening because their mind is elsewhere.

Neither is conducive to you getting a sale, don't outright ask if they have time because that would be a closed question and we all know what happens if you ask one of those too soon don't we. Just use your judgement.

Try not to sound too scripted, it sounds rubbish and people don't respond well to it. Get your practice in and make it sound like a conversation.

Be confident, don't be shy or evasive. It doesn't look good, and it won't come over well. Know your stuff and be ready for the objections (questions)

Change your tone in response to the customer and the reactions they give – monotone isn't much fun to listen to and won't make it sound very exciting.

Don't outright tell a prospect or customer that they're wrong. They might well be but telling them that isn't going to help your cause.

Remember the quote "You may win the battle, but you won't win the war". That's never truer than in this instance. You might win the discussion and prove that you were right, and they were wrong but are you going to now get a sale from them? Unlikely, so why do it.

By the same token, it's not ideal to argue or fight with your prospect or customer for the same reason.

Don't be defensive, they'll wonder why and then you'll lose credibility – never a good plan.

Arrogance comes under the same banner. There's a fine line between arrogance and confidence be very careful not to cross it.

If a prospect wants further info then let them have it. You have nothing to lose except perhaps a brochure or the time it took you to send a pdf on an email to them. But you have everything to gain. That prospect or customer is still in play, they haven't said no so keep on top of it. And by that, I mean follow up on it.

You should treat every lead you get as absolute gold dust. Money will have been spent in some way shape or form to get you that lead so why would you waste it?

When businesses call me to come and train their sales teams, so many of them have databases full of old customers or people who enquired and didn't take it further or the worst ones, prospects who went through the whole of the sales process and then for whatever reason, didn't buy.

Those are, quite frankly, the best (and sometimes easiest) prospects to get in touch with.

You already have their details, and they already know who you are so that's two steps you've already covered in the sales process.

Do a bit of research, try and work out why they didn't buy from you the first time and then offer them something to overcome it.

That's just pain points and the features and benefits.

On another note, if you need to make some sales, try speaking to your existing customers.

I know, sounds a bit obvious, but you'd be surprised at the amount of businesses that don't do it and then wonder why those customers go elsewhere.

Hands down easiest person to sell to is someone who is already a customer.

Why? Because they already trust you enough to give you their hard-earned money so in theory, they should be fairly happy to give you more of it for another product or service that you offer.

Last word of warning, the above will not work if you haven't looked after them as a customer. So many salespeople adopt a 'hit and run' attitude to customers once they've got their money and leave the looking after to someone else. Then when they go back to them to try and sell again, they get some resistance. It takes a lot of time and effort to gain a customer so once you have, make sure you look after them so that they stay as a customer.

To be blunt, cost of sale for acquiring a new customer is much larger than the cost of keeping one. So it pays to look after your customers.

Every business will have to keep looking for new customers because things change, people leave roles and someone new turns up etc.

The good news is that you have in your hands the information you need to build the necessary skills to keep new customers coming in to your business – it's what's generally described as a sales funnel.

I hope that most of this made sense and you're now formulating a plan in your head to sell to your customers, new and old. Remember what we've talked about, practice it and read this book as many times as you need to.

If that's not enough and you'd rather pick my brains personally, we run a **Can't Sell, Won't Sell** course that goes through all the things in this book and more, except that I do it with you and we create something that's personal to you.

If you want to take it that step further then drop me an email and we'll see if we can't get you even more **'Sales Ready'.**

stuart@thesalestrainer.uk

"Great at what he does and a very nice chap to boot. Stuart made it seem so simple. Sales is a bit of a dirty word in my industry... I always thought I was pretty good at getting in front of clients, however a few sessions with Stu and I have seen the light. With the handful of key techniques and phrases he has taught me I have seen a vast improvement in conversion of potential clients. Thank you Stuart". **Simon Jones FPFS**

"Stuart, helped me craft what I wanted to say - using my words in my way and then we practiced and practiced... I am learning so much AND getting sales." **Fanny Snaith - Money Coach**

"Stuart has an aura, an energy, an infectious positivity which makes working with him a genuinely enjoyable experience. This, coupled with his professionalism and knowledge, means that Stuart is a 'go to guy' within his field, who I would have no hesitation in recommending." **Nick Elston, International Speaker.**

The only book you ever need to invest in if you're looking to maximise you or your team's sales potential in the modern business world. Every salesperson starts somewhere. Reading this book won't guarantee success, but it certainly will put them many years further down the path than anyone who hasn't.

Ben Caton, MD at SWSE and Wellmi

Printed in Great Britain
by Amazon

30626699R00066